Breelieve!

A Coloring & Picture Book Featuring Rescue Rooster Bree

By: Camille Licate
Illustrations by: Kate Faehling

Color Your Way to a Better World for All Animals!
Breelieve you can make a difference!
Let Rescue Rooster Bree show you the way!

This book is dedicated to Bree's Grandma Emily and Grandpa Bill.

© 2018 Kids for Positive Change LLC

About Camille

Camille Licate is the Founder and Director of Camille Licate's Kids for Positive Change™, a multi-media educational company designed to reach, teach and inspire kids to take positive action for animals, people and the planet. An animal lover and advocate, Camille launched the Bree and Me Project, with the support of a Pollination Project Grant, to educate kids and adults about the plight of factory farm animals. Through the Bree and Me Project, Camille encourages kids and adults to adopt a "Bree Kind Lifestyle" which includes eating a plant-based diet and using animal friendly and eco-friendly products.

Watching Mom create my coloring book

About Kate

Kate Faehling is an artist and wildlife rehabilitator living in Brooklyn, NY. She has five pets and loves drawing birds, growing plants, and listening to loud music. Contact Kate at dreamcranes@gmail.com

Learn More: breeandmerooster.com
Instagram: @breeandmerooster
Facebook: @breeandmerooster
Blog: breekind.com

© 2018 Kids for Positive Change LLC

A Note from Rescue Rooster Bree

Hi!

My name is Bree! I was lost on a New York City street when I was just 3 days old! I was rescued and brought to Wild Bird Fund, in NYC, where I met my Mom, Camille. She adopted me and we've been together ever since. Mom calls me a "Chicken with a Mission."

Mom and I Breelieve everyone can make compassionate lifestyle choices. This includes adopting a "Bree Kind Lifestyle" by choosing a plant-based diet and eco-friendly and animal friendly products for your homes and bodies.

Will you Bree Kind to All Animals?

Really? Awesome!

With love,
Rescue Rooster Bree

www.breeandmerooster.com
Instagram: @breeandmerooster

© 2018 Kids for Positive Change LLC

Breelieve!

© 2018 Kids for Positive Change LLC

Chick. Love. Happiness.

When I was rescued, I was so small!
Small enough to fit in my food bowl!

© 2018 Kids for Positive Change LLC

Look! I fit in my food bowl.

© 2018 Kids for Positive Change LLC

Did you know chicks are shipped through the mail? A chick is very fragile and should be with its Mother.
I breelieve we can make a positive change!
Please write and call the USPS.
Ask them to stop shipping chicks.

© 2018 Kids for Positive Change LLC

THIS END UP
FRAGILE

© 2018 Kids for Positive Change LLC

Stretch!

© 2018 Kids for Positive Change LLC

Breelax and Enjoy the Moment.

© 2018 Kids for Positive Change LLC

Write and Draw Ways You Can Breelax.

When I was young, I loved a new adventure! I still do!

© 2018 Kids for Positive Change LLC

Adventure Awaits!

Bree Kind to All Animals.

© 2018 Kids for Positive Change LLC

Write and Draw Ways You Can Bree Kind to All Animals.

When I was young, I was so curious. I still am curious!

© 2018 Kids for Positive Change LLC

I learned these are maracas!

What's a rooster to do with a clean pile of towels and blankets?
Roost on them of course!

© 2018 Kids for Positive Change LLC

Roosting lets me rest.

I love my brothers and sister, Ollie, Claire and Teddy Toast.
They are rescues, like me!

In this picture, we are waiting for Mom to give us a treat.

© 2018 Kids for Positive Change LLC

Friends & Family come in all shapes, sizes and species!

© 2018 Kids for Positive Change LLC

I like to stand on the back of Mom's chair and do big wings!

© 2018 Kids for Positive Change LLC

Big Wings Bree!

I was excited to see snow for the very first time!
It was a big change!

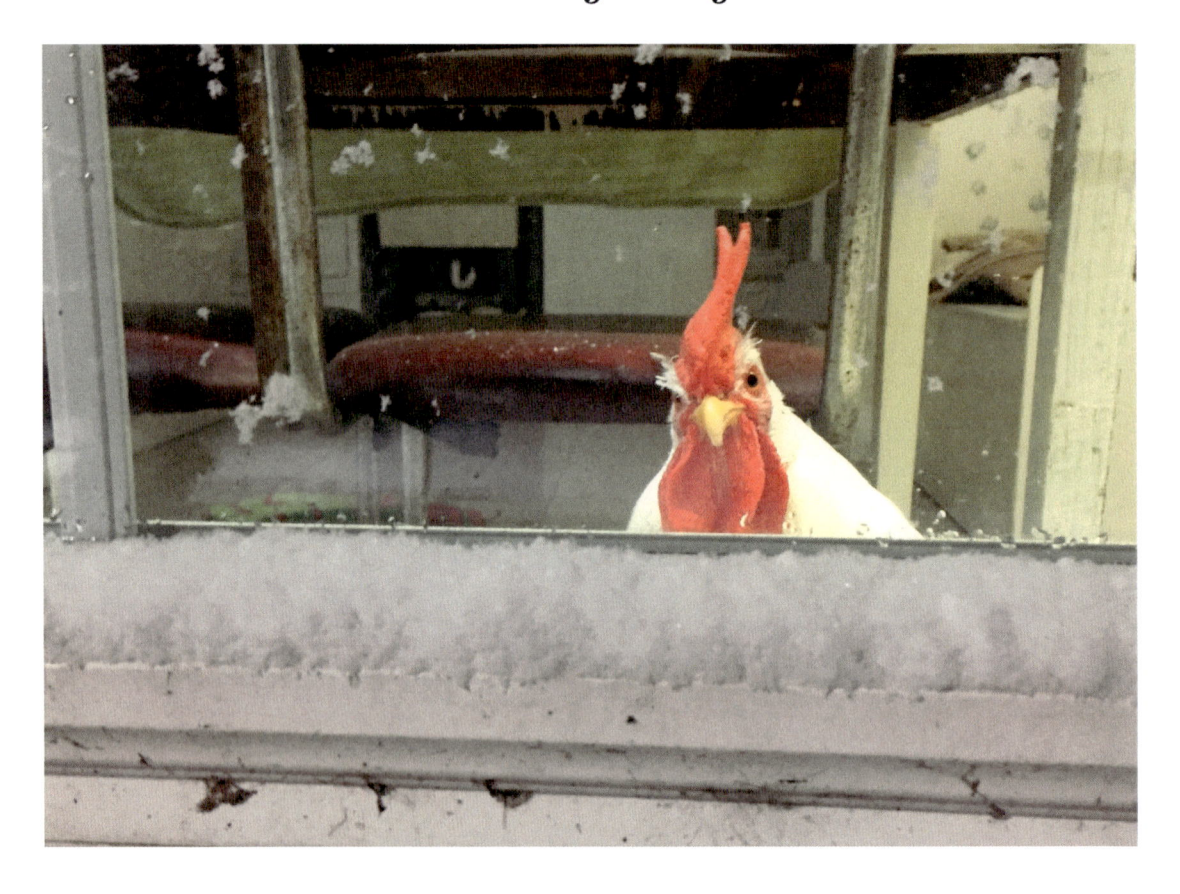

I hope, by getting to know me, it has changed the way you think about chickens.
We are loving, intelligent, protective and curious!

© 2018 Kids for Positive Change LLC

Bree Open to Change!

© 2018 Kids for Positive Change LLC

Are you a Breeliever?

© 2018 Kids for Positive Change LLC

Breelieve You Can Make A Difference!
Bree Kind.

© 2018 Kids for Positive Change LLC

Want to Learn More about a Bree Kind Lifestyle?

Check out these resources:

Leaping Bunny : www.LeapingBunny.org
Minimalist Baker: www.minimalistbaker.com
Compassionate Cuisine: www.casanctuary.org/recipes/
Veg News: www.vegnews.com
Bree and Me Rooster: www.breeandmerooster.com

Special Thanks to:

Wild Bird Fund: www.wildbirdfund.org
The Pollination Project: www.thepolliationproject.org
Microsanctuary Resource Center: www.microsanctuary.org
Institute for Animal Happiness: www.instituteforanimalhappiness.com

To all the men and women working tirelessly to save and protect all animals, from farms to rainforests, deserts to mountains, near and far.
Thank you.

© 2018 Kids for Positive Change LLC

Made in the USA
Columbia, SC
30 May 2019